THE BEAK BOOK

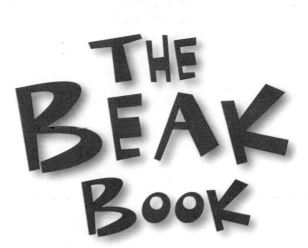

Pamela Chanko

Scholastic Inc.

New York • Toronto • London • Auckland • Sydney

Acknowledgments
Science Consultants: Patrick R. Thomas, Ph.D., Bronx Zoo/Wildlife Conservation Park; Glenn Phillips, The New York Botanical Garden
Literacy Specialist: Ada Cordova, District 2, New York City

Design: MKR Design, Inc.

Photo Research: Barbara Scott

Endnotes: Samantha Berger

Endnote Illustrations: Craig Spearing

***

Photographs: Cover: Michael Fairchild/Peter Arnold; p. 1 & 12a: Wayne Lynch/DRK Photo; p. 1 & 12b: Nigel J.H. Smith/Animals, Animals; p. 2 & 12c: S. Nielsen/ DRK Photo; p. 3: Stephen G. Maka/DRK Photo; p. 4 & 12e: Tom Vezo/Wildlife Collection; p. 5 & 12f: Larry Lipsky/DRK Photo; p. 6 & 12g: R.J. Erwin/DRK Photo; p. 7 & 12h: Frans Lanting/Photo Researchers; p. 8 & 12i: C.C. Lockwood/DDB Stock; p. 9 & 12j: Roland Seitre/Peter Arnold; p. 10 & 12k: Michael Fairchild/Peter Arnold; p. 12d: Stephen G. Maka/DRK Photo.

Library of Congress Cataloging-in-Publication Data
Chanko, Pamela, 1968-
The beak book / Pamela Chanko.
p. cm. -- (Science emergent readers)
Includes index.
Summary: Rhyming text describes beaks of various birds and tells what this part of the anatomy can do.
ISBN 0-590-76969-3 (pbk.: alk. paper)
1. Bill (Anatomy)--Juvenile literature. [1.Bill (Anatomy) 2. Birds.]
I. Title. II. Series.
QL697.C48   1998
591.4--dc21   98-18825
                                                                      CIP AC

8   9   10   08   03   02   01   00

This beak is red. This beak is brown.

This beak is up.

This beak is down.

This beak is open.

This beak is shut.

This beak can peck.

This beak can cut.

This beak is big.

This beak is small.

Two beaks together,

that's 12 beaks in all!

THE BEAK BOOK

Every bird has a bill, which is more commonly known as a beak. Beaks are feeding tools for birds and come in many different shapes and sizes. The shape and form of a bird's beak is a good indication of what that bird eats and how it gets its food.

The cardinal (page 1, left side) has a short, strong beak, which is particularly well suited for seed eating. Not only can the cardinal easily pick up small seeds, but it can also crack them open with ease.

The sharply curved beak of the parakeet (page 1, right side) provides more leverage than the beaks of many other birds, making it easy to crush very hard objects like seeds and nuts. Parakeets also eat insects and fruit.

Robins (page 2) have short, sharp beaks very well suited to ground feeding. They use their beaks to pull up worms, scratch among the dirt and leaves, and uncover insects, snails, and fallen fruit.

The oystercatcher (page 3) lives on the shore and uses its long, strong bill to open the shells of hard-bodied sea creatures like mussels. Sometimes it smashes open the shells of crabs, oysters, and mussels to eat the inside. Sometimes it flips a crab upside down, onto its back, and stabs it with its long beak. Its bill is also well suited to probing the sand and mud for other edible animals.

White pelicans (page 4) use their enormous pouchlike beaks like a fishing net, scooping up large amounts of water. After they drain the water from the pouch (they can hold up to two gallons), they swallow whole any fish that are left.

The spoonbill (page 5) is a large wading bird of shallow waters that uses its long bill, with its broad, flat, rounded tip, to sweep through the waters and filter out small fish and animals.

The northern flicker (page 6) is a type of woodpecker that feeds mainly on ants and other ground dwellers. It crouches and probes the ground with its long, sticky tongue. It nests in the cavities of dead trees, where it also pecks wood, searching for food within the bark.

The bald eagle (page 7), a bird of prey, uses its strong, sharp curved beak to tear and shred its victims, which can then be swallowed.

The toucan (page 8) eats fruit, bugs, and eggs. Its long beak enables it to reach food on thin tree branches that would not be able to support the toucan's weight. It seizes food with the tip of its bill and then tosses back its head, throwing the food back into its throat, where its bristly tongue catches it.

The turaco (page 9) uses its tiny, precise beak to eat fruit. It sometimes swallows berries whole and later regurgitates the seeds.

The crowned crane (pages 10-11) lives in marshland habitats and eats bugs, frogs, toads, plants, and grains. Cranes have powerfully strong bills, which they use like a hammer to kill the small animals they live on.

The next time you see a bird, look at its beak and see if you can figure out what that bird might eat.